A P E R S O

PERSONAL PRAYERS FOR QUIET TIMES

Brief meditations,
with Scripture verse and prayer,
to help people pause a moment
and listen to God

DIMENSIONS
FOR LIVING
NASHVILLE

PERSONAL PRAYERS FOR QUIET TIMES

ISBN 0-687-03800-6

The publisher gratefully acknowledges the use of material prepared as
On the Spot radio scripts by a team consisting of: John Kathage, Rita
Gallasch, Robin Mann, Trevor Reu, George Samiec, Allan Schreiber,
David Schubert, Lance Steicke, Irwin Traeger, Valerie Volk.

Unless otherwise noted, scripture quotations are from the Good News
Bible: Translation in Today's English Version—Second Edition © 1992
by American Bible Society. Used by permission.

Scripture quotations noted NRSV are from the New Revised Standard
Version of the Bible, copyright © 1989 by the Division of Christian
Education of the National Council of the Churches of Christ in the
United States of America. Used by permission. All rights reserved.

GOD IN REAL LIFE

The Word became a human being and . . . lived among us. —*John 1:14*

Most of us heard fairy tales as part of our childhood experiences. Perhaps today our hearts still warm to those fanciful stories of princesses, pumpkins, and enchanted forests.

As cynical adults, we often think that the world of fairy tales still surrounds us—but dressed up nowadays as advertisements, political platforms, and even soap operas. It's a pity when thinking adults place the story of Jesus in that same fairy-tale category. Jesus is no fairy-tale character.

But you needn't take my word for it. Read the Bible record yourself, and you'll find, not a fairy tale, but a man who really loves you—Jesus Christ.

Lord Jesus, thank you for coming and revealing God to us. Amen.

PURPOSE IN LIFE

"I have come in order that you might have life—life in all its fullness." —*John 10:10*

I had a terrible nightmare the other night. I was walking desperately round and round in a massive maze, and it seemed that I was going to be stuck in there forever. It made me feel really scared. I was certainly pleased to wake up and realize it was only a dream!

Real life, for some people, is very much like my terrible nightmare. Many people feel that living is like being lost in a maze—just going round and round with no purpose or meaning, like a rat on a treadmill.

It's wonderful to live with a real purpose, so that each new day is part of an exciting adventure. That's how it is when we live with Jesus.

Lord, fill my life with your love. Amen.

BEING THANKFUL

How good it is to give thanks to you, O Lord.
—Psalm 92:1

A farmer and his family sat down for a meal in a restaurant. Before they ate, they all bowed their heads and gave thanks to God. A fellow diner came over and spoke to the farmer: "I notice you're from the country. Where you come from, does everyone say a prayer before eating?"

After a thoughtful moment the farmer replied: "No, the pigs don't."

Many people forget to give thanks to God for even the simple things of life, like the food we eat. Our God is so good that he gives us our daily food even when we forget to thank him. Why not say "thanks" every day?

Thank you, God, for all the good things you give me every day. Amen.

SAFE WITH GOD

With his own hand he protected me. —Isaiah 49:2

I heard the thunder booming outside last night, and I went out to the veranda to watch the huge forks of lightning streak across the sky. I know that it terrifies some people, and maybe I'd be frightened if I didn't have a house to shelter in. But I like thunder and lightning.

When I see the sky light up, I think how puny our streetlights are and how enormous is the power at God's disposal, and it makes me feel secure. After all, if God is taking care of us, and he's so powerful, what can we possibly be afraid of?

Nothing can hurt us when God's hands hold us close.

Lord, keep me safely in your hands. Amen.

SEEING PAST OURSELVES

We are all joined to each other as different parts of one body. —Romans 12:5

I was in the art gallery the other day when I saw a young man stop in front of a priceless watercolor. I admired his taste. But my impression of him changed when he looked into the glass-covered painting and combed his hair. It seemed as if his reflection in the glass interested him more than the painting.

People who can't see past themselves miss an awful lot. They go about the world without really seeing it.

We *should* look at ourselves, but we need to look to God, too. He's the only one who can help us look past ourselves and see the beauty in others. Why not ask him to help you do just that?

Lord, help me see the potential in other people and be sensitive to their needs. Amen.

More than Fireworks

Because of your light we see the light.—Psalm 36:9

Fireworks displays create an exciting atmosphere! The darkness is lit up with rockets and showers of colorful lights. But fireworks are really rather sad. Just a moment of glory, a splutter, and they're gone!

Some people think life's like that. Just a brief time of energy, color, excitement, and then darkness—nothing!

But they're wrong! Jesus Christ lights up our dark world. Understanding his teachings in the Bible is like light penetrating the darkness around us. We discover his promises of eternal life and life after death.

That'll be a rare display of beauty. The Bible tells us so. And it will last a lot longer than a firecracker!

Lord, you give me light. Show me the way to go. Amen.

PAYING THE PRICE

You know what was paid to set you free.

—1 Peter 1:18

Inflation! Just hearing the word makes you shudder. Electricity, gas, clothes, housing, education—all the things we need for everyday living—continue to rise in price.

We may grumble and complain about these high prices. But they are nothing compared to the price God was prepared to pay to redeem all humanity, including you and me.

He paid the highest price for us. He paid with the innocent blood of Jesus his Son, who died for us. There can be no higher price than that. He did it because he loves you.

Thank you, Lord, for loving me so much that you sent Jesus to die for me. Amen.

THE GIFT OF LIFE

"Those who live and believe in me will never die."

—John 11:26

Recently an elderly woman left me a large, crystal basket in her will. We hadn't been friends for long, but professionally I'd often made tiny baskets of flowers for her to give to others. Now she'd left me with a valuable reminder of happy hours spent chatting about life.

On our last visit together we'd talked, too, about death. Both of us trusted the promises of Jesus when he said, "Those who believe in me will live, even though they die."

It was a gift from him we both treasured, because it promised life after death. It's his will that you receive that promise for your life, too.

Lord, keep me on the pathway to life; for Jesus' sake. Amen.

Gᴏᴅ's ᴘʟᴀɴ

How wisely you made them all!   —Psalm 104:24

Sir Christopher Wren designed a ceiling supported by pillars for the Windsor City Hall, London. Leaders inspecting the finished building thought the ceiling was insufficiently supported, and they ordered more pillars. Wren disagreed. However, he added two more pillars. But they don't do anything—they don't even reach the ceiling.

He created an optical illusion to fool the city authorities. Today, Wren's "illusion" amuses many tourists.

We're often like those Windsor City fathers. We question the design and wisdom of our Creator, thinking to improve on his plans for our lives. Our failure to acknowledge the abilities of the Almighty God would be a joke if it weren't so serious.

Help me trust in you, Lord, for you know what is best. Amen.

Under pressure

Peter went out and wept bitterly. —*Luke 22:62*

He was under pressure—intense pressure. It wasn't that he was a weakling. In fact, he was big and tough. But he cursed and swore, all out of character. The pressure almost had him at the breaking point. You see, they were leading his best friend to the place of execution. And he was scared. He might be the next. And then he denied ever having known him.

Now he could hardly live with himself. He had denied his best friend! And that's why it was such a relief that, when Jesus came out and looked at him, Peter wept—wept bitterly.

They were tears of grief and guilt, but they were also tears of relief. Jesus didn't hold Peter's action against him. He forgave him.

And the pressure was lifted.

Lord, forgive me and restore me; for Jesus' sake. Amen.

GROWING IN COMPANY

All of you are Christ's body, and each one is a part of it.
—1 Corinthians 12:27

We'd been looking for some trees to plant on a block of land we'd just bought. The man at the nursery was very helpful—he reeled off lists and told us the likes and habits of different species.

"Now take this one," he said. "It's a beauty, but you'd have to plant a few. They grow best in clumps—they like company."

We did take a few, and they grew well.

It's not just trees that do best in company; for most of us, our need for others is very real. We need people to love us, people to comfort us, people to share our joys and our griefs.

No wonder God made this a part of his most important command: Love your neighbor as yourself.

Lord, help me love my fellow human beings.
Amen.

THE PRICELESS PEARL

"The kingdom of heaven is like a merchant in search of fine pearls." —*Matthew 13:45 NRSV*

Jewels are fascinating. Tales of treasure troves, tourist attractions (the Hope Diamond, the Crown Jewels)—raw material for the poets.

I like pearls, and it has always intrigued me that Christ compared the kingdom of heaven to a pearl. Then I discovered that pearls were indeed great treasure in the ancient world; in Rome, only upper-class people were permitted to wear pearls, and dealers would spend their whole lives hunting for perfect specimens.

So, when Jesus told his audience about the merchant who found a perfect pearl and sold everything he had to buy it, they would have recognized the story. They would have understood his point that to find God it is worth giving up everything else. God is the priceless pearl we all need to possess.

Lord, help me see that in you I have everything I need or could desire. Amen.

Communication

God has shown us how much he loves us.

—Romans 5:8

Communication often seems so inadequate. *You* say one thing, and *they* hear another.

When I tell my children I don't want them to go to a certain party, they hear me saying that I don't love them and that I'm not interested in their happiness. Sometimes we need to add actions to our words. I need to demonstrate to my children in some other way that I love them and want them to be happy.

When God tells us he loves us, we often hear him saying something quite different. But he has made clear his meaning by his actions. In no uncertain terms, he demonstrated that our well-being is uppermost in his mind.

That demonstration of love was given when Jesus died for us. That's communication that really counts.

Lord, help me always see in Jesus your great love for me. Amen.

A GOD WHO HEARS

He hears me when I call to him.   *—Psalm 4:3*

Have you ever tried dialing your own telephone number? Nothing much happens. Most of the time, you'll get a funny noise or a busy signal. There's not much point in talking under those circumstances. To have a conversation, there has to be someone at the other end of the line.

It's something like that when we pray. Prayer isn't just talking to oneself. There has to be someone at the other end of the line.

And, of course, there is. He's there. And he hears. God is a God who is there. And a God who listens.

You can be connected with the God who is there through Jesus.

Lord, listen to my prayers. Help me ask for things that please you. Amen.

THE LIFELINE

He will cover you with his wings; you will be safe in his care. —*Psalm 91:4*

Kites are wonderful to watch in flight. Yet, remarkably, all that controls them is a thin cord. They swoop and dive—and then climb back up higher than before. Enormous pressures are exerted on them, and they are buffeted by all sorts of destructive winds.

We, too, bravely strive to fly high and fast and as beautiful as we can. Large pressures are exerted on us by all sorts of destructive situations. What control line can we rely on?

God's lifeline for us is Jesus Christ. God's promise in Jesus can keep you safe and flying high.

Lord, keep me safely attached to you, for Jesus' sake. Amen.

Wise planting

Teach me, LORD, what you want me to do, and lead me along a safe path. —Psalm 27:11

We can learn from our mistakes!

A man with a tiny garden planted tomato bushes under his clothesline. The retractable line wasn't extended when he did the planting, but later he found it was possible to hang and dry sheets only on still, sunny days, because when the wind blew, the staked tomato bushes snagged his washing.

Often we fail to take into account the consequences of our actions. We make a mistake in thinking the things we say or do now will have no influence on others later. Sometimes it's too late to correct bad examples given earlier.

May God give me the wisdom to plant tomatoes—and sound principles—in the right place!

Lord, help me know what is right, and give me the power to do it. Amen.

DESPITE THE DROUGHT

My God will supply all your needs.

—Philippians 4:19

Does the sight of stunted stalks of wheat, desperately trying to support ripening heads of grain in the face of hot winds, bother you?

On a trip north recently, I missed the animals bobbing like marshmallows in the green, mint-jelly pastures. Evidence of drought unfolded everywhere. What a refreshing surprise it was to see on a freshly painted sign in front of a little country church: "Despite the drought, we will rejoice in the Lord."

Obviously, these were people who knew the God who made the seasons, and they were prepared to accept hard times when they came. I'm often guilty of taking for granted things that others provide for me.

Lord, help me be thankful for all the good things you give me. Amen.

Nothing to pay!

By the free gift of God's grace all are put right with him through Christ Jesus. —*Romans 3:24*

BUMP! Someone had just run into the back of my car at the traffic light. My heart sank. *Not again!* When the car was new, the same thing had happened when my husband was driving. It had cost a fortune to fix the damage.

Getting out to inspect the scene, I met a smiling face. "Your car's okay, Ma'am—I just dented my bumper on your tow bar." What a relief! No damage done! Nothing to pay!

I get that same feeling of relief with the knowledge that God forgives me. I don't have to pay a thing! He forgives me—for Jesus' sake.

Lord, help me accept in faith and with thankfulness what you have done for me. Amen.

EASTER BUNNIES

*If Christ has not been raised, then your faith is
a delusion.*   *—1 Corinthians 15:17*

The Easter bunny stopped visiting our home years ago. Of course, we love all the traditions of Christmas and Easter, and we observe many of them that have meaning for our family. But to suggest that a rabbit was the bringer of "new life" associated with Easter-egg giving seemed too absurd!

Easter is the time when we remember the triumph of Jesus Christ over death by his resurrection to life. He—not the Easter bunny—gives us the promise of eternal life.

Only a "bunny" would put his faith in anyone else but Jesus, the giver of new life. When we eat our eggs, we remember the facts, not the fiction!

Lord Jesus, you have died and risen to life again. Help me trust only in you. Amen.

Like sheep

"I am the good shepherd."   *—John 10:11*

Sheep are funny creatures. When they are let out of the sheep yard to be taken back to their paddock, you may see one of the first sheep do a little jump as it goes through the gate. Then what happens? You're right! All the other sheep make the same jump as if they had to clear the fence to get out. Sheep will easily follow a leader.

God says in his Word that people are like sheep. Most of us will follow a strong leader.

The best leader this world has ever known is Jesus. He is the Good Shepherd who will lead us into the right pathways of life. Life is wonderful when you can say, "The Lord is my shepherd."

Lord, my Shepherd, lead, guide, and protect me.
Amen.

SEEING INTO THE HEART

LORD, you have examined me and you know me.
                                        —Psalm 139:1

In London there's a building called "The House That Never Was." It has no doorbell or letterbox. Nobody visits. Nobody sits on the balcony. More than a million people have walked by and never noticed anything strange.

It's a fake house painted on a cement wall. It hides the entrance to an ugly subway tunnel, and was painted to blend with nearby homes.

Are we like that house? Do we hide ugliness, loneliness, and insecurity behind a sham front of composure?

Jesus, "the God who *ever* was," sees through outward appearances and looks on our hurting hearts with compassion. Ask him to make you good on the inside.

Lord, you know me as I am. Make me clean and heal me. Amen.

WHAT IS GOD DOING?

"Why have you forgotten me?" —*Psalm 42:9*

God, sometimes you make me so mad! You always seem to be messing things up—wrecking people's lives, spoiling their happiness, leaving behind you a trail of broken hearts and lives.

You don't seem to do what you're supposed to do, either, and you hurt so many people. Some get sick. Others starve. Still others die, often slowly. God, you make me mad!

And you don't even answer me. You're so silent!

The crazy thing is that I still believe you when you say you do care, you are in charge, you want to be involved. I just can't get away from that cross on a hill and that man called Jesus.

Lord, when everything seems to be wrong, help me simply cling to Jesus. Amen.

Written in blood

"Be glad because your names are written in heaven."
                                                —*Luke 10:20*

There were seventy of them altogether—thirty-five teams of two. They were full of excitement when they came back and reported: "Master, we've seen everything. We did great things—in your name." They were excited over their success.

"I can understand your excitement," the Master told them. "But I want you to be excited and happy about the right thing. Don't be excited and happy over what you've done. Rather, be excited and happy because your names are written in heaven."

If your name is written in heaven, it's written there not because of what you have done. It will be written there in blood—the blood of the Master, Jesus Christ.

Thank you, Jesus, for giving your life so that my name is written in heaven. Amen.

LOVING

We love because God first loved us.   *—1 John 4:19*

"Make love—not war," goes the old expression. But what does it mean to "make" love? Beyond the obvious, does it also mean washing dishes, helping to make beds, or getting up at some unearthly hour to clean up the mess made by one of the children when he or she is sick?

We show love in our actions if love is in our hearts.

Love is God's gift to us because he is love. God's idea of loving hits the nail right on the head—the nails that pierced the hands and feet of Jesus.

Lord, help me show your self-giving love to others. Amen.

THE PARTY

Let us celebrate our Passover, then.

—1 Corinthians 5:8

The table was decorated with red roses and blue forget-me-nots for the dinner party. It was a celebration for our friend. He died suddenly—a year ago.

His wife, parents, and sisters joined us. We talked about the day that changed our lives so dramatically. Memories of his thoughtfulness, humor, and influence in a very short lifetime were shared.

Some might think us odd to have a party on such an anniversary. But that's what the Christian church does every Sunday—it celebrates the life and death and new life of a dear friend, Jesus, whose death and life changed everything for us.

Join the party on Sunday! Jesus is your friend, too, remember!

Lord Jesus, help me always remember you and rejoice in you. Amen.

LOVE FOR THE UNLOVELY

"The Son of Man came to seek and to save the lost."
—*Luke 19:10*

I find a lot of people hard to take—people who talk too much or too loud; people who are nasty or greedy; people with bad breath or bad manners; neurotic people or self-centered people.

In fact, apart from a few friends, there are not that many people I'm really attracted to. And let's be honest—most of us are probably more attracted to attractive people.

But Jesus is different from us. He was always attracted to those who were unattractive—the sick, the lonely, the depressed. He lived and died for poor, hurting people—people like you and me— and he still offers to be our companion forever.

Lord, make me more loving, as you have loved me. Amen.

ALL OF US

"I have not come to call respectable people, but outcasts." —Matthew 9:13

He must be a bit odd, I thought—walking into a public meeting wearing one brown shoe and one blue sandal! In professional attire, and with others similarly dressed around him, this man's odd footwear was clearly obvious.

We notice the unusual: the person who dresses strangely, speaks differently, or acts contrary to our expectations. We sometimes make wrong judgments because of these things. For instance, when you break a bone in your foot, it's necessary to wear odd shoes.

I'm glad Jesus found time and understanding for the persons considered by society to be odd. We all are unusual in some way, and yet we all share a certain brokenness of life. How comforting it is to know that Jesus cares for us all.

Lord, help me accept other people, as you have accepted me. Amen.

Happy birthday

Jesus Christ is the same yesterday, today, and forever. —Hebrews 13:8

They stood, lined up behind the birthday cake. The candles flickered, the mothers fussed, the photographer waited patiently.

"Everybody ready? All together now—" And then the click, and it was over.

They sang "Happy Birthday" and blew out the candles, and the cake was carted away for serving. All over! But the camera had captured it for us.

That cake is eaten and gone, those children now are adults, and most would no longer remember that day. But on film it remains, preserved unchanging.

And there is One to whom all our days are known, in whose memory each of our moments is kept, by whom every hair on our heads is numbered: a God who cares.

Lord, as things around me change and disappear, keep me fixed in you forever. Amen.

BEING DIFFERENT

"My thoughts," says the Lord, "are not like yours, and my ways are different from yours."

—Isaiah 55:8

We moved into a new house a few weeks ago. There was the usual chaos, but eventually life returned to normal. Well—almost normal, except for one disconcerting thing: At every sink, bathtub, and shower, the hot and cold faucets were the wrong way around!

Did I say "wrong"? What I really mean is that they're the reverse of normal. It's going to take me a long time to learn that the right-hand tap is hot, not cold. I don't really mind. It's a good idea to be shaken out of patterns and routines sometimes.

Jesus knew this. He challenged people to look at things with new eyes and to think afresh. Read his words in the four Gospels, and see how he challenges us today to think again about our lives.

Lord, help me see things as you see them. Amen.

Beyond the Rise

I will not be afraid, LORD, for you are with me.

—Psalm 23:4

I was driving along a strange road, going up a small hill. I had no idea what was on the other side. The thought suddenly occurred to me: *What if the road suddenly went over a cliff at the top, or into a crater?*

But, of course, it didn't. We take it for granted that our roads are properly looked after and we don't have to worry.

Life is a bit like that. We have a God who loves us and has planned the way for us, even when we don't know what's over the next rise.

Jesus showed us that. He, himself, is the way.

Help me not to worry, Lord, but simply put my trust in you. Amen.

PEOPLE

The Son of God . . . loved me and gave his life for me.
—Galatians 2:20

People fascinate me. I could spend all day watching people walk along the street, if I had the time. I think, *Look at him; I wonder what makes him tick? Look at her. She looks worried.*

People must have fascinated Jesus, too, I think. He certainly had a great love for people. He talked with them, taught them, mixed with all sorts, asked questions, and gave answers. There must have been times when he shook his head in amazement—and sadness—over people.

But that didn't stop his love and concern for them. That's the only possible explanation for his death on the cross—his love and concern for people, including you and me.

Help me, Lord, to show the same love and concern to others that you have shown me. Amen.

Not fair

"He was humiliated, and justice was denied him."

—Acts 8:33

I got mad at my wife this morning! "It isn't fair," I yelled at her as I slammed the door. And she shouted back, "If you think it isn't fair, I think it isn't fair either . . . " But by then I wasn't listening anymore.

I calmed down a little on the way to work. After all, I thought, if ever anyone could have said, "It isn't fair," it was Jesus Christ. He came to do something about the injustice in this world. He got an unfair deal, if anyone ever did. But he took it all.

It may not have been fair, as we count fairness, but in his love, he did it for us.

Lord, make me more patient, for Jesus' sake.
Amen.

GOD WILL HELP

Leave all your worries with him, because he cares for you. — *1 Peter 5:7*

The tear-filled eyes showed that her heart was ready to break. "I don't think I'll ever see my daughter again. She's only seventeen. Why can't they find her? Why doesn't God help me?"

It's a rather frightening experience when it seems that God does not help us, that he's gone into hiding. Some people say that, since God didn't help as soon as they called him, he does not exist at all.

But God is there all the time. He does care. He experienced all our pain and sorrow in Jesus. He knows how to help us, and we may turn to him even—and perhaps *especially*—in our moments of greatest need.

Lord, help me trust in you at all times.
Amen.

Showing the Way

I praise the LORD, because he guides me.

—Psalm 16:7

Stoplights again! I'll be late; have to get to the air-port by 10:00 to meet the boss—hope I'll make it. So many deadlines to meet today—rush, rush, rush.

Yellow lights are on! Better unwind a bit, while I sit here. Relax—let go. God, help me keep calm, help me realize you're in control.

Green light's on!—I'm on the move again.

O God, guide me when I have to make tough decisions. Show me the way today, tomorrow, always. I know you'll get me through in this life. Take me right through into eternity to be with you.

Lord, take my hand and lead me. Amen.

Found!

"'I am so happy I found my lost sheep. Let us celebrate!'" —Luke 15:6

The big tears belonged to the eyes of a little boy about four years old. "What's wrong?" I asked.

He replied, "I'm lost. I can't find my dad."

It's easy for a little boy to get lost in a huge shopping complex, especially on a Saturday morning. It was marvelous to see his eyes light up and his face beam with smiles when we finally found his dad.

There are a lot of grown-up people who've lost their heavenly "Dad." When you have that empty, lost feeling in your life, it could be because you've lost your God.

Let God find you. Your eyes, face, and heart will beam with joy.

Thank you, Lord, for searching me out and finding me when I was lost. Amen.

IN FULL CONTROL

My help will come from the LORD, who made heaven and earth. —Psalm 121:2

I magine that on a jet flight, this announcement comes over the intercom: *Good morning! You are part of a historic flight. This is the first completely automated airplane. No human being is in control. We want you to relax and enjoy your flight. We want to assure you there is absolutely nothing to worry—worry—worry—worry . . . !*

As we speed through life on this whirling planet, is there someone at the controls, or are we in the hand of blind fate?

I think there would be good reason for panic if there were no God in control of this universe. Jesus said, "Do not worry, your Father in heaven is in control. Put your trust in him."

Lord, help me not to worry, but to put my trust in you. Amen.

INNOCENT SUFFERING

Even though he was God's Son, he learned through his suffrings to be obedient.   *—Hebrews 5:8*

A friend of ours got fired from her job yesterday. We just didn't know what to say. We were angry; we don't believe she deserved that kind of treatment.

But then, neither did Jesus deserve death on the cross; he hadn't done anything wrong. We feel anger that he should have had to suffer like that, although he was quite innocent. However, there was a purpose behind his innocent suffering—to free us from sin.

There doesn't seem to be any silver lining behind our friend's loss of job. What we've been able to remind her is that Jesus knows what it's like to suffer innocently, and she knows that he cares for her.

With you, Lord, I can face any troubles. Help me share your comfort with others. Amen.

THE EXCHANGE

It was while we were still sinners that Christ died for us!
—Romans 5:8

Ten men were condemned to die! It was during the Second World War, in a German concentration camp. One of them had a young family. A Catholic priest offered to take his place. Even the hardened prison guards were amazed as the exchange took place.

That priest died instead of the young father.

You know, that reminds me of what God did for me, for you, for everyone. We could never do enough to deserve such a gift. But Jesus died instead of us, to make us his friends, and to give us life—life now and forever.

Thank you, Jesus, for dying in my place.
Amen.

ACCEPTED

The person who loves God is known by him.
—1 Corinthians 8:3

If you saw me on the bus each day you'd only give me a passing glance. I'm just like any other office worker—on the surface.

But I know what I'm like inside. Often I didn't like what I saw there. Sometimes it all got a little much for me, and I couldn't see why anyone should like me.

Then I came across a man who loves me even though he knows my inside story. He makes me feel really worthwhile. Now I can live with myself—even *like* myself.

That man's name is Jesus—I read about him in the Bible.

Lord, help me accept and love others as you have loved me. Amen.

FRIEND

...e my friends." —*John 15:14*

The noise of an ambulance siren always sends a niver down my spine. A friend of mine was carried off in an ambulance one day, and I lost him. Since he passed away no one else has been able to fill that emptiness in my life.

Some people have lost Jesus. He was their best friend. Even if they try to forget Jesus, the emptiness is always there until he returns.

Have you lost Jesus as your friend? He's looking for you.

In the Gospel of Matthew, Jesus said, "Seek, and you will find" (Matthew 7:7). That's God's promise.

Lord Jesus, stay with me and in me forever.
Amen.

Seeing Clearly

"He controls the times and the seasons."

—Daniel 2:21

For two years I've struggled to read the telephone directory. Now, new bifocals have made everything clear to me.

Yesterday, I thought I was going blind. Today, I can see really well. Depending on which lens I look through, it's possible to see close, tiny detail, or look up ahead to view the horizon.

Seeing what is coming in the future can also be a problem. Violence and disaster seem to obscure future hopes. I'm glad Jesus gave advice about not worrying about tomorrow.

As I read God's Word, I see that he has a vision for my future, and it's not at all gloomy. In fact, it's great.

Guide me, Lord, in the way you want me to go.
Amen.

Message from the King

In these last days he has spoken to us through his Son.
—Hebrews 1:2

A letter from Buckingham Palace! She could hardly believe her eyes. Dated 1918, it was a simple, handwritten expression of encouragement and gratitude from King George V to a faithful soldier who had endured hardship as a prisoner of war.

The daughter of this officer discovered the letter when cleaning out an old trunk recently. Now she has framed it as a reminder of the thoughtful, personal care of a king for those in his service.

The King of heaven, too, gives you words of encouragement for life—signed and sealed with the death and resurrection of his Son, Jesus.

The Bible is a letter from the King to you! Read it and see how he cares!

Thank you, Lord, for caring so much for me.
Amen.

A SIGN FOR OUR TIMES

May God, the source of hope, fill you with all joy and peace. —Romans 15:13

Red letters, spray-painted two feet high on the factory wall, proclaimed the message: "Be negative—not just a blood group, but a way of life!"

I thought the slogan was pretty clever. And it didn't really surprise me, because there's plenty to be negative about—pain, boredom, injustice, spiteful people, unemployment, war, disappointments of every kind.

With all that, it wouldn't be surprising if even God were negative about us and the way we've messed up his world. But he isn't.

Instead, God has put a sign saying "yes" to each one of us, a sign made of flesh and blood. Jesus is the sign I live by.

Lord, help me not to get discouraged, but to take heart in Jesus, my Savior. Amen.

Humpty Dumpty

Lord, heal me and I will be completely well.

—Jeremiah 17:14

Humpty Dumpty sat on a wall,
Humpty Dumpty had a great fall.
All the king's horses and all the king's men
Couldn't put Humpty together again.

It's true, isn't it? Once an egg's broken, all the experts in the world can't do much about it. Humpty Dumpty's a "dead egg"—broken, smashed.

It may sound funny, but people are like Humpty Dumpty. Relationships are broken, and we seem as helpless as a smashed egg. The only difference is that people have a God who is greater than all the king's horses and men—and that's the King himself, the Creator. He can put things together again.

Lord, when my life seems to be coming apart, put me together again. Amen.

CHASING THE RAINBOW

Jesus said to him, "Follow me."   *—Mark 2:14*

I know a man who is one of those people who are forever chasing rainbows. If there were a gold rush somewhere, he'd be off. His life is one mad scramble after happiness. But he never seems to find it. It's always just around the corner. And, of course, it *is* always "just around the corner."

Happiness is an elusive sort of thing. It's not a commodity you buy or find. If you chase happiness, you won't get it. It will always be the pot of gold at the end of the rainbow.

If you chase Jesus, things are different. Happiness comes as a by-product for the person called to follow Jesus, come what may.

Help me, Jesus, always to follow you. Amen.

Stop the World!

God loved the world so much that he gave his only Son.
—John 3:16

Some years ago a popular song said, "Stop the world, I want to get off!"

It expresses a form of escapism, I suppose. It's also a commentary on the kind of world we live in. It is a mess! We may as well be honest about it. When you think of the greed and selfishness, the bitterness and hatred, it's enough to make anyone want to get off.

With Jesus it was different, though. He saw the greed and selfishness and everything else, and he said, "Hey, stop the world, I want to get on! I'm going to do something about it."

And, of course, he did. He gave his life for it.

Help me, Lord, to accept your love and share it with others. Amen.

BEYOND FEELINGS

Even if I go through the deepest darkness, . . . you are with me. —*Psalm 23:4*

A few months ago I heard the news that a very close friend of mine has cancer. Terminal cancer! It left me feeling angry, confused, helpless, and—yes—hopeless.

I'm a Christian. I believe in God, and I believe Jesus is Lord and is in control. But it didn't alter my feelings. I felt so mixed up.

I can't help my feelings. I get scared and upset and angry. I feel helpless and hopeless at times.

It is then that I need to remember him who is greater than my fear and feelings. It is then that I need to look to Jesus, on whom our faith and our future depends from beginning to end.

Lord, have mercy, and be with me. Amen.

In WEAKNESS

What seems to be God's weakness is stronger than human strength.   *—1 Corinthians 1:25*

He was an old man, shuffling along the hospital corridor, a walking stick in one hand, a hat in the other. Just an old man who would seem to some to be not very alive anymore. He's—well—*old!*

Yes, he is, but you haven't seen him smile at his wife, and you haven't seen them kiss. You see, she's dying, and their time together is very precious. His legs may have had it, but his love certainly hasn't.

So let's not be too hasty in judging people like him. So often in life it's the ordinary person who turns out to be a real hero. The ugly duckling turns out to be a swan.

And the man hanging on the cross turned out to be Jesus, the God of the whole universe.

Lord Jesus, be with me in all my weaknesses and troubles. Amen.

An Impressive Sign

What seems to be God's foolishness is wiser than human wisdom. —1 Corinthians 1:25

Now, here's a business card designed to impress: shiny royal blue lettering on a light blue background. The name and address are clearly marked in an elegant copperplate style. The simple but striking logo is in one corner, the phone number in another.

Obviously this is a company with flair and imagination, a company on the move.

You could have taken a page out of their book, God, and designed a much more impressive business card.

I mean, the birth in the manger, the miracles, and the stories Jesus told—they're not too bad. But the logo—a man being hanged on a cross!

What am I to make of it? Help me understand.

Thank you, Father, for sending Jesus to die on the cross for me. Amen.

In Spite of What I Am

Nothing can separate us from his love.

—Romans 8:38

We were driving home, talking about all sorts of things. The kids were fighting a bit. I was yelling. A typical family scene! That's why it was all the more startling when twelve-year-old Helen said, "I liked it when the minister in church said, 'There's nothing you can do to stop God from loving you.'"

It had struck me, too. And I recall thinking: *Now, that's good news if ever there was good news. No strings attached. Nothing I have to do. No goodness required on my part. God loves me, no matter how I am. In fact, God loves me in spite of myself. There's nothing I can do to stop God loving me.*

Yes, I thought, *that's some good news all right!*

Thank you, Lord, for loving me even though I don't deserve it. Amen.

JUST AN ACCIDENT?

By his blood we are now put right with God.

—Romans 5:9

I saw an accident on my way to work this morning. *How on earth did it happen?* I asked myself. *Was he asleep? Didn't she look?*

Come to think of it, why do any accidents occur? Is God in accidents? Does he reach down, twist the wheels of this car, divert that plane, lead a tornado to hit a town?

Then I realized that those were the wrong questions. More important than *why* is our response to accidents.

Was the crucifixion of Jesus an accident? Was it the biggest human mistake ever made? I need to know why this happened. I need to know very specifically what God was doing for me in that death on the cross.

And when I do, I will respond.

Thank you, Jesus, for dying in my place, so that I can live with you forever. Amen.

Snake in the grass

You alone, O LORD, keep me perfectly safe.

—Psalm 4:8

I had a close encounter of the worst kind recently. A brown snake uncoiled and reared its ugly head to stare at me! My arms were full of useless objects, leaving me completely defenseless. "Snake!" I yelled in panic.

Equally startled, the reptile glided away into high grass. My legs felt like jelly!

Common sense should have warned that a hot sun and high, dry grass provided the perfect environment for reptiles.

Not unlike that snake, sin in my life rears its head when I'm enjoying innocent fun. I thank God for a conscience that constantly warns of moral and spiritual dangers ahead.

Lord, keep me safe despite temptation. And when I do fall, continue to forgive me. Amen.

GOD'S SPECIAL GIFTS

Jesus said to him, "Take care of my lambs."
                                              —John 21:15

He's nine years old, but he looks only about six. He laughs and cries, but he doesn't talk. He walks and runs in a clumsy kind of way, and his eyes wander a bit. Society says this boy is disabled, retarded—and perhaps he is. He'll certainly never read or write.

But he is a unique person, and he has a special place in our community. I don't believe he's a mistake, or one of God's cruel jokes. Rather, he's been given to us to be our friend and our teacher, showing us how to trust and inviting us to care for his special needs.

He is one of God's special gifts.

Lord, teach me to care for all people. Amen.

Seeing clearly

Grace and truth came through Jesus Christ.

—John 1:17

When we saw Ayers Rock, we didn't see it glowing orange-red at sunrise or sunset. We didn't even see a sunrise or sunset. What we saw was rain—two inches of it—and clouds hovering around the rock, shrouding it in mystery, giving us only glimpses of its real glory. In its own way it was beautiful, but we couldn't really see it properly.

Like the mysterious, cloud-covered rock, God gives us small glimpses of himself in the world. But it's only when the Son appears, only in Jesus, that we see God clearly. He shows us God's real beauty in giving his life for his friends.

Lord God, thank you for revealing yourself in your Son, Jesus Christ. Amen.

DON'T BE AFRAID

The Lord is with me, I will not be afraid.

—Psalm 118:6

He's so extroverted, and his laughter is so infectious. He's talented, too—reads well and has a great ear for music.

But he has a fear—a terror of having his face under water. Why? No one knows. But it holds him back from really enjoying pools and beaches as much as he could.

Well, which of us isn't like that in some way—afraid of people or heights or new experiences? It's no wonder the phrase "Don't be afraid" keeps popping up in the stories of Jesus. He knows that fear is one of our great enemies. So he says to us, *I'm with you; I take care of you—don't be afraid!*

Lord, reassure me that because of your love and protection I have nothing to be afraid of.
Amen.

Hanging on

I cling to you, and your hand keeps me safe.
                                          —Psalm 63:8

I was standing at the counter of the local deli when I felt a small hand grab my jeans. Looking down, I saw a toddler hanging on to me. She wasn't mine, but I didn't want to scare her by telling her. Luckily, she let go before she even noticed she had the wrong legs, and I saw her wander back to her mother.

We're a lot like that—often grabbing at the wrong things, thinking that they are what we need or that's where we belong, when really it's you, Jesus, that we should be grabbing on to.

Help us, God, to hang on to the right pair of jeans.

Lord, don't let me put my trust in anything else. Amen.

Be still!

We will not be afraid, even if the earth is shaken.
—Psalm 46:2

The storm was terrifying! The lightning flashed! Writhing, turbulent clouds billowed across the sky. Trees, tortured by cruel winds, screamed in pain. Their torn limbs fell bleeding to the ground. The tender earth seemed to groan in sympathy, helpless to relieve the suffering trees.

Suddenly, as if in answer to a great command from heaven, the clouds began to break up, to scatter and flee like hoodlums racing from the streets. The sky cleared. The stars came out and sparkled again. A huge yellow moon sailed calm and serene across the soundless sea of space.

Peace was restored.

God will surely restore peace after our storms of life are over. "He restores my soul" (Psalm 23:3 NRSV).

Keep me safe with you, O Lord, until the storms of life are over. Amen.

As we grow old

Lord, I put my hope in you; I have trusted in you since I was young. —Psalm 71:5

The older woman could barely shuffle along as she clung to the railing in the hallway of the retirement home. I helped ease her into a chair alongside mine.

It was then I noticed she was blind. I wondered whether this old soul would be filled with the bitter complaining of old age, or whether she would be gentle and peaceful.

Her face wrinkled with a big smile as she said, "I can't see God's beautiful creation anymore, but I can hear his beautiful music and talk to my dear friends. I'm just living day by day until Jesus takes me home. Then I'll see God."

What a beautiful way to grow old!

Lord, help me trust in you throughout my life.
Amen.

THE PASSPORT

He opened for us a new way, a living way.
—Hebrews 10:20

Take half the clothes and twice the money," people will say when a trip overseas is mentioned, "and don't lose your passport!"

Plans for the trip of a lifetime are many: vacation time from work to get approved; luggage and clothes to select; bills to pay; mail delivery to postpone; passports to arrange. The list is endless.

There's one trip we'll all make one day. It requires a special passport, but there'll be no hassles with luggage, clothes, or money.

Faith in Jesus is our passport to heaven when we die. Christ paid for the trip with his life. We can go just as we are, trusting him to be our passport for entry into eternity.

Don't lose *your* passport!

Lord Jesus Christ, help me cling to you alone.
Amen.

WAITING

Rejoice! . . . The Lord is coming soon.
—Philippians 4:4, 5

Nine months—for nine months we've waited for our first grandchild. Now it's sixteen days overdue! We know a baby's there—the pulsing evidence looms large before us. But somehow we must wait patiently for the child to come. We're more than ready and willing to love this new member of our family.

Waiting like this reminds me of something else. Jesus says that he will come again on a day that no one knows. His coming is eagerly awaited by those who trust him as Savior and God.

In fact, he's coming whether we're ready or not! You know—we're excited about his coming, too!

Come, Lord Jesus! Amen.

God wants you to keep listening every day to what he says to you in his Word.
Read the Bible, apply it to your life, and respond in prayer and thanks.

OTHER
PERSONAL PRAYERS
BOOKS

Personal Prayers
Personal Prayers for Growing Christians
Personal Prayers for Women
Personal Prayers for Children
Personal Prayers for Teens
Personal Prayers for Graduates
Personal Prayers for Teachers
Personal Prayers of Christians
Through the Centuries
Personal Prayers in Times of Grief
Personal Prayers in Times of Illness
Personal Prayers for Families
Personal Prayers for Seniors
Personal Prayers with Jesus